Pacific Natural
Everywhere

jenni kayne

Pacific Natural *Everywhere*

Photography by Michael P. H. Clifford

New York · Paris · London · Milan

From Marc Appleton

It is a joy living much of our lives comfortably inside while also looking at and venturing outside, especially when the scenery is so inviting. The houses in this book are contemporary yet seductively rural, and the scenery outside ranges from majestic mountains to ocean views.

Intimately composed courtyards, decks, porches, and the occasional lawn sometimes interconnect the two, but more often than not the landscapes here are not overdesigned—they reflect the natural context of a native wilderness and embrace the architecture.

This makes for a wonderful dynamic between inside and outside. Windows frame striking views of nature and doorways open enticingly, and sometimes expansively, creating a tranquil confusion between inside and out. There are many claims for architecture appreciating nature, but with the examples Jenni Kayne has assembled here, what these architects and landscapers and their clients have accomplished is quietly consistent: Simple, beautifully restrained architecture is the best frame, nature is the best picture, and in this elegantly edited book we get to enjoy both together.

Between Indoors *and Out*

Nature has always been my greatest source of inspiration. Growing up in California and now raising my kids here, I feel lucky that a connection with nature is woven into our days. Those small moments of grounding are incredibly important to me—like having dinner with my family outside, pausing to enjoy each other's company, and the beauty of the place we call home.

Over the years, I've become curious about what exactly defines California living and how that idea translates to the spaces we create. To me, it's about ease. Letting nature lead. It's about light and calming tones and spaces that always look out onto nature. Designing a home that supports your daily life in a way that feels natural. When the ethos of California living is at the center, a space invites connection—between indoors and out, between people, and with the natural world around us.

That relationship between interiors, architecture, and nature is what inspired this book. It builds on the first two installments of Pacific Natural, which focused specifically on California interiors and lifestyle. This time, we expand our lens—exploring California as a feeling rather than a place. We test the idea that it can be evoked everywhere, as long as nature dictates design, indoors and outdoors blend, and the seasons shape how we live. In every house we visited, it was that harmony between design and landscape that made it feel like California.

We saw this connection all over the world—from the calm waters of Puget Sound to a colorful valley in Colorado to a rolling beach in New Zealand to the open sky in Wyoming. We also saw how the surrounding landscapes shaped the sensibilities of each house, giving them a true sense of place. To honor that, we've organized the houses by their defining natural elements: aspen, oak, pine, and ryegrass.

As you discover these pages, I hope you feel both grounded and transported to places that evoke that California way of living. And more than anything, I hope this book offers a fresh perspective on the role nature plays in your life, whether you're cooking dinner with the windows open, spending time in your garden, or simply enjoying the view. Everything is connected—and there's so much beauty in that.

CHAPTER 1

With leaves that shimmer in the wind and colors that mark the passage of time, aspens share a beautiful synchronicity with these houses—each one embracing life through the seasons.

ASPEN

Telluride, *Colorado*

Designed with a green roof covered in grasses and wild flowers, this house by architect Jacob Segal nearly disappears into nature. White oak paneling and dark accents match the landscape, while expansive windows frame stunning valley views—drawing the outdoors in like living works of art.

Shou sugi ban siding and Belgian bluestone counters reference the house's exterior.

LANDSCAPES
Georgia O'Keeffe

The overall inspiration draws from the work of Peter Zumthor, Norwegian stave churches, and the rugged beauty of the Dolomites.

A MYCOLOGICAL FORAY
CHICAGO

The garden has flourished over time, carefully tailored to Telluride's climate and local wildlife.

Jackson Hole, *Wyoming*

What's unique about this Wyoming house by Messana O'Rorke is its thoughtful orientation, which offers glimpses of rustic scenery at every turn. From the plush seating in the great room to the Adirondack chairs on the back landing to the glass-wrapped indoor spa, each space comes with a grounding new perspective.

The outward-facing layout takes its cues from the wide-open geography of Jackson Hole.

RT STILIN

Mormon Row—a nearby landmark known for its simple, utilitarian structures—inspired the house's pared-back form.

Minimal landscaping creates an untouched feel and complements the casual interiors.

CHAPTER 2

In mature pine forests, stillness and shade are abundant. These houses are reflective of that—with simple forms and materials that recede into the trees.

PINE

Arrowtown, *New Zealand*

Lush takes on whole new meaning at this house by Pete and Paul Rogers, with garden design by Suzanne Turley. Layered landscaping creates softness and depth, while a grass tennis court rolls continuously into the surrounding hills. Anna-Marie Chin's understated interiors act as a quiet backdrop, keeping the focus firmly on the verdant scenery.

The garden is arranged in tiers—with a pool raised over the natural pond—for a touch of natural whimsy.

The surrounding landscape served as the ultimate point of inspiration.

Melides, *Portugal*

With a concrete exterior in the exact shade as the surrounding dunes, this house by Vincent Van Duysen is a visual extension of Portugal's raw beauty. Brazilian *ipe* wood walls, brutalist furnishings, and a neutral palette create an interior that feels simple yet striking. High ceilings and accordion doors expand the space, letting in light and shadow from every angle.

The low-slung form allows it to disappear into the rolling hills and surrounding cork trees.

The interiors are sparse in furniture but rich in warmth and character.

Brown terra-cotta tiles are a nod to Portuguese tradition.

The mood of each room subtly transforms as the light shifts from sunrise to sunset.

Longbranch, *Washington*

On the shores of Puget Sound, this cabin by Olson Kundig could almost pass as part of the landscape. The modular layout carefully weaves through the forest, with materials that reflect its surroundings—spruce panels in the bedroom mirror the tall pines, river rocks flow seamlessly onto the bathroom counter, and walls of glass let nature take center stage.

The original structure was built in 1959, standing at a modest fourteen-by-fourteen feet.

Silver galvanized columns and beams catch the daylight, mirroring the sparkle of the bay.

Walls of glass blur the distinction between indoors and out.

CHAPTER 3

Defined by their deep roots and longevity, oaks lend a sense of strength to the spaces tucked beneath their canopies.

Los Angeles, *California*

Whether it's the perfectly imperfect charcoal-colored brick or the wild, canyon-inspired garden, this house by Marmol Radziner offers a grounded connection to the earth. Dark materials give the interior a moody elegance, while skylights and windows bathe everything in natural light. Together, the effect is quietly immersive—rooted in nature yet open to the sky.

The contrast between the light exterior and darker interior makes the surrounding greenery appear even more vivid.

Exterior zinc panels create a sense of continuity and openness.

Each room features a thoughtful combination of skylights, glass doors, and windows.

Big Sur, *California*

Perched high above the Pacific, this Big Sur retreat with the design and landscape by Mark Haddawy is equally rustic and refined. By famed architect Will Shaw, the house is built almost entirely from salvaged redwood—from the floors to the ceilings to the wraparound deck—to create a warm sense of cohesion. The generous scale only heightens its elemental quality, with exposed beams, sparse furnishings, and wide-open rooms.

A twelve-foot Bertoia sound sculpture makes a striking first impression in the entry.

Floor-to-ceiling windows in the bedroom filter light like trees in a forest.

The outdoor hot tub surround was constructed from found stones.

Los Angeles, *California*

Though just minutes from the city, this canyon retreat by Vincent Van Duysen feels worlds away from Los Angeles. Limewashed brick-and-white-oak floors ground the design, while linen seating and Scandinavian furnishings add softness. In the living room, sliding glass walls open fully to the landscape by Christine London, effortlessly bringing the outdoors in.

The property's oak trees dictated the house's layout.

Dark window frames add definition and draw attention to the surrounding landscape.

A stone fountain and striped loungers create a casual backyard retreat.

Soft grasses were planted as an homage to the canyon's native landscape.

CHAPTER 4

Known for its resilience and ability to thrive in open terrain, ryegrass sets the tone for these houses—each one unfussy and rooted in simplicity.

RYEGRASS

Mangawhai, *New Zealand*

Built by Fearon Hay with interiors by myself, this coastal retreat epitomizes indoor-outdoor living. In the great room, glass walls vanish, opening to a central courtyard on one side and sprawling lawns on the other, with details perfected by Suzanne Turley. Outside, a minimalist cabana sits among the dunes, overlooking a pool that looks nearly natural.

Warm whites and soft linen upholstery create a sense of calm against the lush landscaping.

A dark stone coffee table anchors the living room and is paired with collected ceramics and a modernist hanging sculpture.

Undulating sand dunes stretch out into the distance, adding to the setting's ethereal quality.

Mangawhai, *New Zealand*

Situated between the Pacific Ocean and a pine forest, this cedar-clad cabin by architects Fearon Hay and designer Sonja Hawkins is designed for both ease and connection. A farmhouse-style kitchen table doubles as a gathering space, while built-in nooks invite conversation. In all directions, generous outdoor spaces create a sense of home within nature.

MARAE

A wood-burning fireplace, leather furniture, and New Zealand wool rugs bring true coziness to the space.

Intimate seating areas tucked within larger rooms help balance the house's scale.

Bathroom details include aged brash finishes and a view to the outdoors.

NOTES

Resources

Telluride (p 18)
Architect: Jacob Segal
Interior Design: Saree Kayne and Jacob Segal
Landscape Design: Saree Kayne

Jackson Hole (p 42)
Architect: Messana O'Rorke
Executive Architect: Shawn Ankeny of Ankeny Architects
Interior Design: Messana O'Rorke

Arrowtown (p 64)
Architect: Pete and Paul Rogers
Interior Design: Anna-Marie Chin
Landscape Design: Suzanne Turley

Melides (p 82)
Architect: Vincent Van Duysen
Interior Design: Vincent Van Duysen
Other Mentions: SIA Arquitectura

Longbranch (p 104)
Architect: Jim Olsen
Interior Design: Jim Olsen
Internal Collaborators:
Brent Rogers (Project Manager, 1981)
Ellen Cecil (Project Manager, 2003)
Derek Santo (Architectural Staff, 2003)
William Franklin (Project Manager, 2014)
External Collaborators:
Tom Harris (General Contractor, 1981)
Steve Clark (General Contractor, 1997)
Mark Ambler (General Contractor, 2003/2014)
Brian Hood Lighting Design (Lighting Designer, 2003/2014)
MCE Structural Consultants (Structural Engineer, 2003/2014)

Los Angeles (p 124)
Architect: Marmol Radziner
Interior Design: Marmol Radziner
Landscape Design: Marmol Radziner

Big Sur (p 140)
Architect: Will Shaw
Interior Design: Mark Haddawy
Landscape Design: Mark Haddawy

Los Angeles (p 166)
Architect: Vincent Van Duysen
Interior Design: Jenni Kayne
Landscape Design: Christine London

Mangawhai (p 190)
Architect: Fearon Hay
Interior Design: Jenni Kayne
Landscape Design: Suzanne Turley

Mangawhai (p 216)
Architect: Fearon Hay
Interior Design: Sonja Hawkins
Landscape Design: Philip Smith of O2 Landscapes

Thank You

To my mom—thank you for exposing me to the most beautiful outdoor spaces around the world and for dragging me to garden and design tours from a very young age. Your love of gardens has been one of the deepest inspirations behind this book.

To my dad—thank you for being my number one supporter and for always trusting me with so much creative freedom in your own homes. Being able to design spaces for you and mom to enjoy is one of my greatest joys.

To my husband, Richard—thank you for being the most incredible partner and father. You constantly challenge and inspire me. I'm so grateful you found us our dream property; it's been such a joy to watch it grow and evolve with the seasons, our family, and our ever-expanding menagerie. I feel so lucky to have met my Virgo match—whose eye is as discerning as mine.

To Rip, Tan, and Troop—you fill our home and garden with so much energy, love, and life. Being your mom is the greatest gift, and you inspire me every day to create spaces that reflect the beauty of our time together.

To my friends—thank you for your constant inspiration, encouragement, and love.

To my sisters—thank you for always believing in me, trusting me, and inspiring me with your support and your beautiful homes.

To my Jenni Kayne team—I'm beyond grateful to all of you. Thank you for your tireless work and for making it all look effortless and perfect, always with smiles on your faces.

Katherine, Lauren, and Meagan—thank you for bringing this book to life. Capturing this California sensibility—beautiful architecture set in stunning natural landscapes—was a dream of mine, and you made it come true. Making this book with all of you has been such a gift. I'm so grateful for your eyes, your hard work, your commitment, and your infectious laughter.

To Michael—thank you for capturing such beautiful images, often across the world and even on your own vacations. Your eye and artistry have brought this book to life in the most extraordinary way.

To Christine London—thank you for creating my dream garden. Working with you to celebrate my surroundings in every aspect of my home has been such a joy. I am forever grateful for your eye.

Mark Appleton—thank you for writing the perfect foreword. I'm grateful for your kind words and your ability to capture the magic I hope this book conveys. I couldn't imagine a better voice to introduce my third book.

To Ellen Nidy, Charles Miers, and the team at Rizzoli—thank you for your trust and unwavering support. I'm honored to be creating our third book together and deeply grateful for this continued creative partnership.

To the homeowners, landscape architects, designers, and architects featured—thank you for inviting us into your exquisite homes and sharing your magical projects so generously.

CREATIVE

(Jenni Kayne, Lauren Berle)

PHOTOGRAPHY

(Michael P. H. Clifford)

PHOTO ASSISTANT

(James Messina)

PRODUCTION

(Camille Ulam, Rayne Simmonds, Jacqueline Weeger)

VOICE & CONCEPT

(Jenni Kayne, Katherine Shpall)

DESIGN

(Meagan Hubin)

COPYWRITER

(Giana León)

STYLING

(Sarah Peddicord)

First published in the United States of America in 2026 by
Rizzoli International Publications, Inc.
49 West 27th Street, New York, NY 10001
rizzoliusa.com

Foreword: Marc Appleton
Copywriter: Giana León
Photographer: Michael P. H. Clifford

Publisher: Charles Miers
Editor: Ellen Nidy
Design: Meagan Hubin
Production Manager: Colin Hough Trapp
Managing Editor: Lynn Scrabis

2026 2027 2028 2029 2030 / 10 9 8 7 6 5 4 3 2 1

Printed in China

ISBN: 978-0-8478-7628-0
Library of Congress Control Number: 2026710207

The authorized representative in the EU for product safety and compliance is Mondadori Libri S.p.A., via Gian Battista Vico 42, Milan, Italy, 20123, www.mondadori.it

Visit Us Online:
Facebook.com/RizzoliNewYork
Instagram.com/rizzolibooks
Youtube.com/user/RizzoliNY